I Want to Be a Scientist Like

ORVILLE & WILBUR
WRIGHT

WRITTEN BY VICKI AHLSTROM

ILLUSTRATED BY MITCH BAIRD

"Here boys, CATCH!" Wilbur and Orville Wright's father had just returned from a trip. He threw their gift into the air.

The boys ran to catch the toy, but it didn't fall!
It twirled up, then slowly came down.

Wilbur and Orville had so much fun with their new toy. It was made of only wood, paper, and a rubber band, but it could fly. They made more toys like it and experimented with them.

The brothers were always making things or taking machines apart to see how they worked. They built all kinds of kites to fly.

As they got older, they became better at inventing.
They made their own printing press to print newspapers.

Wilbur needed a quicker way to fold the papers,
so he invented a folding machine.

When bicycles became popular, Wilbur and Orville opened a bicycle shop. They fixed bikes and even invented their own.

8

Wilbur and Orville were a good team. They shared ideas with each other and were good at solving problems.

They began working on a problem no one else had solved yet—how to make a machine that would fly.

They read what other inventors had tried.
They experimented with kites and gliders.
They worked for years and didn't quit.

Finally, together, they built the first airplane that really worked. Others learned from them.

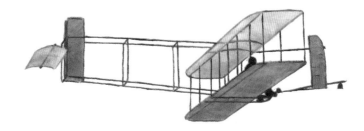

Today we have jets, rockets, space shuttles, and there are more things yet to be invented. But it all started with two brothers who had great ideas and never gave up.

WILBUR WRIGHT   ORVILLE WRIGHT
(1867–1912)   (1871–1948)

Businessmen
Wilbur and Orville Wright started a printing business and a bicycle shop.

Scientists
They researched and conducted many experiments with gliders.

Inventors/Fliers
The Wright brothers built and flew the first successful motorized plane at Kitty Hawk, North Carolina, in December 1903.

They produced the first military airplane and made many great contributions to the science of flight.

"We were lucky enough to grow up in an environment where there was much encouragement to children to . . . investigate whatever aroused their curiosity."